Maid of Heaven

Maid of Heaven

The Story of Saint Joan of Arc

By

Ben D. Kennedy

RLK PRESS

Maid of Heaven
The Story of Saint Joan of Arc

RLK Press

www.MaidofHeaven.com

ISBN 0-9752-6562-8
Library of Congress Control Number 2009929385
Printed in the United States of America

*To Jehanne d'Arc
and to God Who created her*

*M*ost beautiful maid of Heaven,
how brilliant is your light.
Like a shining star, you point the
way to the Father of all light.
Praise be to Him for sending you
here to show us how to fight.

*T*ho born just a lowly peasant girl in
an out of the way place known as Domremy.
'Twas you alone with the courage to
answer God's call to set your nation free.
Only sixteen when you left home for good,
you little knew your life's true destiny.

1

*W*hat must you have thought when Voices first came and told you all that God wanted done. St. Michael, St. Margaret, St. Catherine all telling you the same message: you were the only one Who could rescue your oppressed people from the English and unite all of France as one.

*O*beying your Voices, you went to the nearby city of Vaucouleurs to ask for help in God's name. But their leader, Robert de Baudricourt, sent you back home, refusing to believe in your claim. Had he not heard what the prophecies foretold: France must be saved by a maid from Lorraine.

While de Baudricourt refused you, others stepped

forward, like Jean de Metz your faithful knight.

On his honor he pledged to lead you to the King,

so you could help Charles reclaim his birthright.

You told him you should leave: "Today rather than

tomorrow, tomorrow rather than in a fortnight."

Back to de Baudricourt you swiftly went,

because your Voices told you he would finally relent.

You pleaded with him to send you, because you

knew you must be with Charles before mid-Lent.

Another battle had been lost by the French, and

he must understand all that the loss truly meant.

3

A great loss had indeed occurred, as you foretold near Orleans at the Battle of Rouvray. When the news reached de Baudricourt, he at last was convinced and sent you on your way. As you left the town, he waved and yelled at you: "Go then maid, and let come what may!"

*O*n to Chinon to see the King; or rather the Dauphin, as you felt he should properly be called. Never officially crowned as King, it was part of the mission for which you had been called. To lead Charles to Reims for his coronation and anointing, so that he would be legally titled.

*T*he other part of your mission, raising the siege at Orleans, had to precede the coronation. For this, you needed full support from Charles as well as from the rest of the French nation. So you made the hard journey to Chinon, sustained by the Spirit and filled with anticipation.

*U*pon reaching the city, you were eager to see Charles but were told you must instead wait. The King and his court advisers were unsure about trusting in you and your heavenly mandate. Finally, they agreed the King should at least see you after almost two whole days of debate.

As they escorted you to the great hall of the palace, what was going through your mind? Just a country girl from a small town about to meet some of the greatest of all human kind. But you had been sent from God, and merely knowing that gave you your peace of mind.

As you entered the court, Charles had devised a test by hiding himself among the crowd. Led by your Voices, you quickly found him out, fell to your knees and reverently bowed. Greatly impressed, he agreed to speak with you in private away from his usual crowd.

6

*A*lone in the royal chamber, you were able

to give him the answer to his earnest prayers.

That he really was the legitimate heir to France's

throne, despite all of his mother's affairs.

Through Jehanne the maid, he could have faith

this was what the King of Heaven declares.

*C*harles was still cautious and wanted more

proof, so he had you fully examined to be sure.

First at his castle by several ladies of his court,

to see if you were indeed physically pure.

Then questioned by church theologians at

Poitiers, which was much for you to endure.

7

*T*hey wanted to know every minute detail

about your life, and if in God above all you relied.

They questioned why you needed an army, if

God truly desired to deliver the French side.

"In God's name, the soldiers will fight and

He will grant victory," you emphatically replied.

*F*or three weeks, they continued their questioning,

and you thought they would never relent.

They asked for you to give them a sign before

they gave you their full blessing and consent.

Exasperated, you declared: "Send me to Orleans,

and I'll show the sign for which I was sent."

8

*F*inally, the day came when they gave their

approval and officially sent you to fulfill your mission.

To Tours, you proceeded to be outfitted with all

that was required by your new martial position.

There, you were given a suit of white armor, so

you would be seen in the best of military tradition.

*A*s for a sword, your Voices knew best,

telling you where St. Catherine's could be found.

At her Church, you had them look behind the

altar for a sword buried beneath the ground.

Inscribed with five crosses and covered with rust

that fell off; yes, the right sword was found.

*M*ost importantly, you needed a banner so everyone would know you when you held it up high. White field with lilies, proclaiming "Jesus Maria" and showing God sitting in judgment in the sky. Beautiful to behold, the message was clear that for victory in God alone you would always rely.

*A*t last, the time had come for you to join the army that you were predestined to lead. At Blois, you found them to your great dissatisfaction committing many a moral misdeed. "It is not enough that God be with us, but we must be with God," you were forced to plead.

10

*O*nce made chaste by your shining example,

the army marched toward Orleans as planned.

What a procession it must have been, with

singing priests leading the way for four thousand.

Gleaming in your armor while holding your

banner, you cheerfully exhorted your command.

*A*pproaching Orleans was where you first met

Lord Dunois, who was to become a loyal friend.

Your first words to him were harsh, for his changing

your route, a decision he tried hard to defend.

"In God's name, the counsel of God our Lord is

safer and wiser than yours," you did contend.

If Dunois was offended, he quickly forgot as your mere presence seemed to help turn fate around. The Bastard, as he was called, thought bad winds would prevent crossing the river into his town. As soon as you spoke, the wind changed direction; an event Dunois felt added to your renown.

You desired to remain with your army, but the desperate people of Orleans would not be denied. For seven months, they had been besieged by the English, with little help from the World outside. As you entered the city, the people began cheering, believing their deliverer had finally arrived.

12

You wasted little time going to work; first warning the foe of their peril, if they chose to defy. You shouted for Glasdale, the English commander, to surrender, or he would most surely die. Defiantly shouting back many obscenities and calling you profane names was their only reply.

With victory assured by the counsel of your Voices, you favored a most aggressive attack. Your captains were less confident, scheming among themselves for a way to hold you back. "You have been at your counsel, and I have been at mine," you argued in support of the attack.

*T*he next day, May 7, 1429, would be long and hard, but would end with spectacular success. You asked Father Pasquerel to always stay near your side, so he could aid you in your distress. "Tomorrow blood will flow from my body, above the breast," to the father you had to confess.

*W*ith great courage, you led in attacking the Tourelles, the strongest fort the English possessed. As you had predicted, at about midday you were pierced by an arrow, just above your left breast. In great pain, you wept as they carried you to the rear for the bad wound to be properly dressed.

14

Without you in the lead, the army quickly lost confidence and the offensive ground to a halt. As daylight dwindled, your captains became discouraged, and decided to call off the assault. Making a miraculous recovery, you regained your white banner and yelled to renew the assault.

Tho tired from battle, the men were overjoyed at seeing your full resurrection from the grave. Renewed with a sense of victory from your seeming invincibility, they became incredibly brave. Charging with reckless abandon, the fort was overwhelmed by the fury of their attacking wave.

*I*nto the Tourelles, you went with your men,

as the fleeing English tried their best to retreat.

"Glasdale, Glasdale, submit, submit to the King

of Heaven," you would passionately entreat:

"I have great pity for the souls of your people

and yourself." But he refused to admit defeat.

*T*rying hard to escape, Glasdale fell through the

burning drawbridge, and drowned in the river.

It became a complete victory as the rest of the

defenders were either killed or forced to surrender.

Far from rejoicing, you were moved to tears for

the souls of the men you would always remember.

16

*T*he next day, the English decided to abandon

their remaining siege line and leave without delay.

Your army was eager to fight again, but you

restrained them, knowing what was best on that day.

"In God's name, they are going; let them leave,

and let us go give thanks to God for it's Sunday."

*I*n only three days, you had relieved a siege

of seven months and set the city of Orleans free.

The French leaders had asked for a sign, and you

had given one that the entire World could see.

To Orleans' people, you were rechristened; to them

the Maid of Orleans you would forever be.

17

As the French nation rejoiced, you stayed focused on completing what remained of your mission. Leading Charles to Reims, to be crowned King, was the most important part of your commission. To get to Reims, your army had to fight through miles of enemy territory against stiff opposition.

Along the way, you were able to fulfill a promise you made to the good Duke of Alencon's wife. At Jargeau, the Duke was standing in harm's way when you told him to move or he'd lose his life. Your "beau duc" was thus spared from a cannon ball that hit where he'd stood during the strife.

18

*A*s your army moved forward, you continued to lead with the help of your prophetic insight. Time and again, your army would need reassurance that the outcome would turn out all right. Always you encouraged them to "strike boldly," because in God's great hands was the fight.

*A*t Patay, the battle began in much the same way as most did during the entire Loire campaign. Your captains were cautious in the face of the enemy and went to you for counsel once again. "You will have need of good spurs to chase after them," you had wittingly tried to explain.

19

*E*ncouraged by your words implying victory,

your captains became aggressive and attacked.

*A*ided by providence, LaHire and his cavalry

overwhelmed the English before they could react.

*A*s panic ensued, the English were routed and

slaughtered in a defeat having a portentous impact.

*P*atay was a mirror image of Agincourt, the

battle your French remembered as their worst day.

For nearly fourteen years, the shame of that

terrible loss had taken all their confidence away.

*N*ow you had restored French national pride,

while achieving your greatest victory at Patay.

20

*W*ith the road to Reims cleared, the time to

officially crown Charles as King had finally arrived.

In the great cathedral of Reims, he took his oath,

with you standing with your banner at his side.

Your mission completed, you embraced the new

King's legs, looking up at him as you cried.

*N*oble King, now is accomplished the will of

God," you proudly told him through tears of elation.

Just months earlier, you proclaimed you would

save Orleans and lead Charles to his coronation.

Now you had fulfilled all you had promised, and

would forever be a hero to the French nation.

*B*ut as you celebrated at Reims, did you know you were already at the height of your success? Did you remember your own dire warning: "Use me well for I shall last but a year more or less." Whatever you knew, you kept it well hidden, for at this moment you showed no sign of distress.

A march to Paris seemed the logical next step to you, but was this where God wanted you to go? Surely, your calling included cleansing all of France, but for once, you did not seem to fully know. With your Voices silent, you did what you thought best, and rescuing Paris was clearly apropos.

22

What you were unaware of was that Charles had

adopted a different plan that favored negotiation.

Corrupted by unscrupulous advisors like Trémouille,

the King no longer had the same motivation.

All the advantages you had gained him in the

preceding months were lost through his hesitation.

The English and their French allies the Burgundians

were only too happy to agree to a short truce.

Promising peace, they reinforced Paris, taking full

advantage while Charles was behaving obtuse.

With your pure heart, you were never able to

understand why the King was so easy to seduce.

23

With Paris secured, the English and the Duke of Bedford dared you to break the truce and fight. "Come on, pretty maid!" proclaimed their banners as they marched forward with all their might. You were ready to "come on" and give battle, but your King had refused to give you the right.

Charles perhaps thought he could pacify you, by acceding to the only request you'd made. You had asked him to exempt Domremy from taxes, in order to give the people there aid. The King failed to understand that you could never be corrupted by any worldly accolade.

24

When the Burgundians did not surrender Paris at the end of the truce, you were ready to invade. But when Charles agreed to yet another truce with Burgundy, you knew you had been betrayed. Feeling your true loyalty was to God and the French people, you would no longer be delayed.

With Alencon, you rode to St. Denis, to survey the Paris defenses before the great offensive. Knowing you had to fight not only the enemy but also treachery must have made you pensive. Without a clear message from God and support from the King, were you also apprehensive?

25

*B*ut what else could you do except try to lead France forward by liberating its greatest city? As always, you personally led your men forward to the walls, inspiring them by being gritty. After a harsh day of heavy fighting, it was you alone that kept the army battling for the city.

*A*s darkness overtook the battlefield, so it seems you were also finally overtaken by the night. A crossbow through the thigh brought you down and caused most of your army to take flight. Dark forces had finally beaten you at Paris, and would now try to fully extinguish your light.

26

*U*nwilling to accept defeat, you pleaded with your remaining captains to renew the assault. Alencon and a few others still believed in you, but the King intervened and ordered a halt. Utterly dismayed, you left your white armor at St. Denis, knowing the loss was not your fault.

*I*n the ensuing months, the King and his corrupt advisors had tried to limit what you could do. The army was disbanded, and to Alencon, Dunois and LaHire you were forced to say adieu. Never again would you be allowed to lead these knights, who had always stayed loyal to you.

27

*T*he King, sensing your distress, tried to appease you by rewarding your service to the nation. You received armorial bearings of a sword supporting a crown with two fleur-de-lis in formation. You were elevated to nobility and named du Lys (flower of France); an appropriate appellation.

*C*harles may have been quite genuine, in saying "thank you" for all that you had done for him. Or perhaps he was just trying to keep you loyal, at a time when your future looked so grim. All that mattered to you was that God had chosen him, so you would always be loyal to him.

28

*T*hroughout the winter, as you remained at court, you were like a caged eagle seeking flight. In the spring, your chance came when cities petitioned Charles for rescue from their plight. While you were given only a tiny army, it must still have pleased you, once again free to fight.

*A*round Easter, your Voices informed you that you were to be captured by St. John's Day. You knew your time was limited, but when the message arrived, did it cause you great dismay? God would aid you, so you were to accept it and understand it had to happen in such a way.

29

You begged to be allowed to die, rather than taken prisoner, but your Voices were insistent. God had a plan, and you were to acquiesce completely and trust in Him, and not be resistant. And so you obeyed, though facing a future that would make even the bravest a little hesitant.

When the city of Compiègne cried out for help, you went there to give your "good friends" aid. On May 23, 1430, you left the walled city for what would be the last sortie that you ever made. When the drawbridge was raised in your face as you tried to reenter, you must've felt betrayed.

30

Fighting to the last, as the enemy closed in

from every side, you tried your best to get away.

Finally pulled from your horse, amidst shouts

of "Surrender!" you refused to yield in any way.

"I have already surrendered to God," you told

them, knowing He had preordained this day.

To the Burgundians who captured you, there

was no greater prize of war they could attain.

As fellow French who had long opposed you,

they looked at you with both awe and disdain.

Now that they had you, they rejoiced, celebrating

what they considered to be their great gain.

31

*A*s a prisoner of war, you had the same hope as any POW that you would regain your freedom. You could have been rescued by your own countrymen, or even freed by payment of a ransom. If only Charles had been more loyal; but alas, his sole care was for himself and his kingdom.

*T*o your English enemies, your capture was the great opportunity they had been waiting for. They knew they could never allow you to be free again, if they wanted to finally win the war. Their desire was to destroy you completely, which is why they called you a witch and a whore.

32

JEANNE D'ARC

1430

*S*cheming with corrupt church leaders loyal to

the English, Bedford decided what he would do.

If tried by the Church for witchcraft, you would

be killed and your name would become taboo.

In this way, Bedford thought he could reverse all

of the great victories that had been won by you.

*W*hen you heard you had been sold to the English,

you must have known what your fate would be.

They had always told you that if ever they caught

you, they would promptly burn you for heresy.

Facing such a terrible end must have made you

desperate to find your own way to become free.

33

You made several attempts to escape, the most daring being a jump from a tower sixty feet high. Later you simply explained that: "Rather than be in the hands of the English, I preferred to die." The attempt failed as they found you unconscious, and took you back to your tower in the sky.

Injured from the fall, you were comforted by St. Catherine, told to confess and have more belief. The town of Compiègne would be rescued by St. Martin's Day, she told you to your great relief. But hearing you must see the English King before being delivered just caused you more grief.

34

Truly, I do not want to see him," you told St.

Catherine. She only repeated what you must do.

You had to accept your fate, for it was God's

will, and He would aid you and see you through.

Hearing this must have greatly tested your faith,

knowing what the English were likely to do.

The day you had long dreaded finally arrived,

as your sale to the English was consummated.

Ten thousand francs was the blood money paid

for the right to be able to have you eliminated.

Sold away in a manner similar to your Lord, did

you then realize all to which you were fated?

*U*tterly alone, you were marched away on a winter journey in what was the winter of your life. Guarded by coarse soldiers who did not even speak your language, your hardships became rife. Did you wonder what your life might have been if you had just stayed home and been a wife?

*A*s you traveled along, the English were busy preparing Rouen to be your final destination. Leaving nothing to chance, they hand-picked judges that would engage in little deliberation. Headed by Bishop Pierre Cauchon, who had proven English loyalty by previous collaboration.

*T*echnically, you were now a prisoner of the

Church, so you should have been guarded by women.

But even after reaching Rouen, you remained

guarded by soldiers whose treatment was inhuman.

A clear violation of Church rules that Cauchon

would have rectified, had he been an honest man.

*B*ut Cauchon was not an honest man, and he

had sold his soul to govern in your sham trial.

Tho he went to great lengths with his "beau

procès," to provide for himself plausible denial.

The truth is readily seen in his actions toward

you that were always harsh, extremely hostile.

37

*B*efore your actual trial began, Cauchon had your background investigated while you waited. His agents went back to Domremy, to secure evidence from witnesses that were interrogated. Failing miserably, "Nothing was found we would not wish to find about a sister," they stated.

*C*auchon also sought to destroy you by having you physically examined in regard to your purity. Despite a constant threat of rape from your guards, you had somehow maintained your virginity. Another blow it was in his efforts to formulate an accusation; but still he proceeded with alacrity.

38

*A*fter months of preparation, the trial finally got underway with your official summons to appear. A simple young girl standing alone before fifty learned ecclesiastics, you must have known fear. "Answer boldly, and God will aid you," your Voices had told you to help you overcome the fear.

*C*auchon began by requiring you to swear to answer all the questions that they would ask you. Remembering the counsel of your Voices, you refused, which caused Cauchon's face to turn blue. Explaining, you told him: "I can not swear because you may ask me things I must not tell you."

As a great tumult broke out in the court,

Cauchon continued demanding for you to swear.

Remaining defiant, you told him you would swear

concerning all you had done in getting there.

But as to your revelations from God, they were

private, and not for you to publicly declare.

A fter a long debate, Cauchon finally gave in,

allowing you to take the oath your own way.

Kneeling down and placing both your hands

on the Bible, you swore as one would pray.

In such a way, your trial began, with you

showing the strength they desired to take away.

40

Jeanne d'Arc devant ses juges

*S*tarting with simple questions about your background, they tried their best to get you to stumble.

Standing firm, you questioned their authority, as their violation of Church rules was undeniable.

"I should be in a church prison guarded by women," you demanded knowing they were liable.

*T*he day closed with Cauchon demanding and you refusing in a replay of how the day began.

He tried to forbid you to escape, but you would not be bound by only the word of such a man.

"It is true that I have wished to escape. It is lawful for any prisoner to try to escape if they can."

*C*auchon realized after the first day that you
would be harder to convict than he had thought.
For future questioning, he would use Jean Beaupère,
who could make any defendant distraught.
Highly skilled in verbal exchange, he would twist
your words no matter how hard you fought.

*I*n case that was not enough, Cauchon also
employed spies in your prison cell to gather evidence.
Nicolas Loiseleur disguised himself as a fellow
prisoner from Lorraine to gain your confidence.
Learning he was a priest, you confessed to him,
believing your words would be held in confidence.

42

You should have realized that Loiseleur was nothing more than a snake sent to you to deceive. But being daily chained and mistreated in your prison cell had weakened your ability to perceive. Also forbidden as you were from Church worship, you were probably just desperate to believe.

Returning to court day after day under such constant torment was bound to take a heavy toll. Continuing daily to try to make you swear the way they wanted weakened your self-control. "You are burdening me too much," you told them, not understanding it was exactly their goal.

43

*Y*our judges employed a rapid-fire method of questioning, designed to fatigue and confuse. "Where were you born? Why do you wear men's clothes? What language do your Voices use?" "Please ask one at a time," you innocently responded, unable to understand this subtle ruse.

*I*n between the seemingly harmless questions, you were asked a question designed to ensnare. "Do you know if you are in God's grace?" was the impossible trick question asked by Beaupère. Astounding him, you said: "If I am not, may God put me there; if I am, may God keep me there."

44

*Y*ou also confounded your judges by refusing

to answer certain questions, replying "Pass on."

Still they persisted in getting you to reveal more

about your saints' roles in your commission.

"I answered these questions at Poitiers," you

said, referring to the Church's first examination.

*T*he higher court at Poitiers had affirmed your

mission, so you thought they should understand:

"I came into France at God's command, and I

have never acted except at God's command."

Cauchon was well aware of Poitiers, but would

not allow it to interfere with what he'd planned.

$\mathcal{P}$roceeding as if the subject of Poitiers had never been brought up, the questioning began anew. "Were you able to see your saints?" to which you responded: "I see them as clearly as I see you." They further asked you if your saints had hair, and you replied: "It is good to know that they do."

$\mathcal{G}$rowing weary of senseless questions, your patience waned as reflected in your answers below. When asked what sign you gave to Charles: "Send for him, and perhaps he will let you know." When asked if you would accept a dress: "Give me one, and I will take it and go; otherwise no."

46

The questioning continued like this, until

Cauchon realized he needed a more effective way.

Choosing his most ruthless judges, he reconvened

in your cell, where you were easier to sway.

Alone with such men, you should have realized

that they only looked upon you as their prey.

They tried to get you to admit your Voices were

not from God, for failing to better protect you.

You replied that your capture was the will of

God, and your saints would never betray you.

You were to be saved by a "great victory," and

nothing your saints ever told you was untrue.

*T*hey demanded to know why God would send his saints to speak to you, a simple country maid. You told them God had great pity for France, because her people cried out to Him as they prayed. "It pleased God to defeat the enemies of France, and drive out the English through a simple maid."

*T*hese judges claimed they were the Church Militant, and as such, you were required to submit. Having trouble understanding the terms Church Militant or Church Triumphant, you would admit: "It is my sense that it is all one, God and the Church, and there should be no difficulty about it."

48

*S*uch simple and pure faith should have

impressed them but these men only saw weakness.

Persisting in their demand that you submit to

their authority, you grew tired under the stress.

"Take me to the Pope in Rome and I will submit

to him," you answered them, to their distress.

*Y*ou were within your legal rights to appeal

to the Pope, so your trial should have ended.

Cauchon became extremely angry, ordering the

official record be stricken and amended.

"Ha, you write whatever is against me, but

will not write what is for me," you contended.

49

*F*inally beginning to understand how corrupt your judges were, you issued them a warning. "You say you are my judges; I know not if you are or not, but take great care in your judging. If you judge me badly, you will put yourselves in great danger; I have done my duty in telling."

*C*auchon, believing there was enough evidence, had the formal articles of accusation printed. Seventy charges in all, with your refusal to submit to the Church Militant the most serious listed. As they read it aloud, your heart must have sunk, hearing how your answers had been twisted.

50

With the deck stacked as it was, Cauchon realized his bias would not be completely ignored. By offering legal help from a judge of your choice, he thought he could balance the record. You declined, saying: "I thank you, but I have no wish to abandon the counsel of our Lord."

Cauchon was pleased that he had been able to create a legal basis to condemn you to the stake. But he knew he still needed to get you to say believing your Voices came from God was a mistake. Only your own denial would prove your actions evil and imply the king you had crowned was fake.

*I*n order to compel you to say exactly what was desired, Cauchon was even ready to torture you. Angrily, you screamed: "If you were to tear me limb from limb there is no more I would tell you! If I did say anything, afterwards I would always declare I was made to say it by force from you."

*R*ealizing physical torture would be useless; Cauchon schemed with his judges for another way. They decided that only the threat of burning you to death would be enough to get you to sway. Your faith was pushed to the very limit, as they forced you to face the fire on the 24th of May.

52

*C*onvening in the cemetery of Saint-Ouen, the

spectacle was designed to be extremely gruesome.

Wheeling you out in a cart in front of a hostile

audience, you still looked innocent and winsome.

But mounting a stage across from one with your

judges must have made you feel very loathsome.

*Y*our judges resumed pressuring you to deny

your Voices and submit totally to their authority.

You remained defiant, saying you would only

submit to God in Heaven or the Pope in his city.

The Pope was too far away, they answered,

demanding you submit to the present committee.

53

*T*hey started screaming at you, "Abjure, abjure!"
but you did not understand what that meant.
They defined it as an admission of all your crimes
as charged, and a promise you would repent.
Threatening to burn you if you refused, they incited
the crowd, which just added to your torment.

*T*hroughout your life, you had shown superhuman
strength, as you had acceding to your capture.
But you were after all only human, and as we all
do, you had a limit to what you could endure.
Finally, the temptation of church prison verses
burning was too much, and you agreed to abjure.

54

There is no doubt you little understood what you had done having been compelled under duress. Hearing you were saved and would be readmitted to the Church may have eased your distress. You told them to take you away, to be among women, where you agreed you would wear a dress.

Your hope of being treated justly must have evaporated when you heard what Cauchon next said. Despite his promise to send you to a church prison, he ordered you taken back to your cell instead. Knowing he would never keep his word to you must have made you wish you were already dead.

*W*as it later with your saints that you became aware of the true consequence of your abjuration? To save your life, you had damned yourself by denying the truth about your divine inspiration. Your Voices admonished you to confess to God, and ask Him for forgiveness and restoration.

*Y*ou knew they were correct, because written in the Bible is the Lord's warning to his own: "For whosoever will save his life shall lose it," caused you a pain you had never before known. What follows: "Whosoever will lose his life for my sake shall find it," gave you hope to atone.

56

*K*nowing what you had to do, it probably mattered

little that Cauchon was devising another snare.

Cauchon knew if you resumed male attire, he

would still be able to burn you in Rouen's square.

Telling the English: "I will catch her yet," he laid

for you a trap only one so perverse would dare.

*A*dvising your guards they could do as they

wished, he knew it was your rape they would pursue.

Your sole protection had been your male clothes,

so he also knew what you were likely to do.

Only you know completely the horrors you endured

for three days and all that was done to you.

57

*C*onveniently laid out on the third day were

the clothes you had been forbidden from wearing.

Finding you in these clothes, they accused you of

not abiding by what you promised in abjuring.

"I would rather die than remain in this prison,"

you answered, revealing your deep despairing.

*Y*our judges asked if your Voices had returned,

and you replied that they had, to your relief.

Reminding you again of abjuring, you replied

that ever since then you had suffered great grief.

"I only said what I did out of fear of the fire,"

adding you had never departed from your belief.

58

They told you by continuing to believe in your

Voices, you condemned yourself to the flame.

"I have faith in God and none in you," was

your honest reply to these men with no shame.

"There is nothing more for me to do here!

Send me back to God, from Whom I came!"

Cauchon was ecstatic and informed his English

masters: "Be of good cheer, the deed is done."

Knowing he could now pronounce you a relapsed

heretic, he celebrated believing he'd won.

All that was left was the formal procedure, and

to oppose him he knew there would be no one.

*T*hree days later, official word arrived, and you learned you were to die by being burned. "Alas! That my body, clean and whole, and never corrupted, must today to ashes be turned. Ah! I would much rather have my head chopped off, seven times over, than to be burned!"

*S*eeing Cauchon, you yelled to him: "Bishop, I die through you," which must have chilled his soul. Agreeing you could have Holy Communion, he must have tried to ease his conscience for his role. At least in your final hours, you once again enjoyed the Church's mercies in preparing your soul.

60

*A*s you entered the valley of the shadow, did

you glimpse eternity, and begin to understand?

Did you realize the deliverance your Voices had

promised was your death, now close at hand?

And the victory they had promised was your

martyrdom; it was to be just as God had planned.

*M*ay 30, 1431, was to become one of the very

darkest days that the World has ever known.

Transported to the pyre in a cart, wearing a long

white gown, you appeared as a white stone.

This tragic scene of you being led to your execution

must have caused all of Heaven to groan.

61

S ome of your judges, in viewing, were overcome

with remorse and asked for your forgiveness.

The snake Loiseleur, convicted by his own guilt,

ran out to your cart lamenting his wickedness.

Even a few of the English had tears in their eyes,

and later admitted it was a horrible business.

Y our destination reached, you dismounted,

and began to pray as few had ever heard before.

Invoking God in submitting your spirit, your

words took flight, where your soul desired to soar.

You asked God to forgive your judges and the

English; an act of mercy impossible to ignore.

62

You mounted the platform, continuing your

concern for others, even with you own death so near.

"Rouen! Rouen! Must I die here? Ah, Rouen, I

fear you will have to suffer, because I die here!"

You would finish as you had always lived, thinking

little for yourself in a life completely sincere.

You asked to be given a cross, knowing you were

only moments away from your own crucifixion.

An English soldier crafted one with two sticks,

which you kissed for strength to end your mission.

A priest also retrieved one from a church, and held

it up level with your eyes during the execution.

63

*A*s the flames grew higher, you told the priest to

"go," fearing he would burn or die from the smoke.

In pain we can only imagine, you never ceased

crying out to God for the help you tried to invoke.

Appealing to Him, Who could best empathize:

"Jesus, Jesus, Jesus!" were the last words you spoke.

*A*nd so your life ended, but it was not the end

but rather the beginning of your immortal light.

As with your Lord's own death, agents of darkness

celebrated, believing they had won the fight.

Soon they realized that instead of extinguishing,

they only caused you to shine forever bright.

64

*I*n the aftermath of your execution, almost

everyone in Rouen realized they had burned a saint.

An English soldier, adding to the fire at the instant

you cried "Jesus!" cursed his lack of restraint.

Seeing a white dove fly away that very instant,

he began raving over and over: "She was a saint!"

*Y*our executioner told your judges: "I am

damned, I killed a saint! God will never forgive me."

He explained that in spite of all his efforts,

your heart refused to burn, a real miracle to see.

Thus, your legend grew, eventually bursting

through the darkness with the truth for all to see.

*A*lthough you were alone at the end, you were

not forgotten by your country or the people there.

LaHire and some of your old troops had planned

to rescue you but arrived late to their despair.

And your mother Isabelle Romée never gave up

petitioning God for justice thru her daily prayer.

*T*he English had thought that once you were out

of the way, they could again resume their advance.

You had warned them what would happen, but

they thought killing you would give to them France.

As you foretold, Paris was liberated, and in 1450,

the English were completely driven from France.

66

*W*ith the English gone, Charles, out of either

remorse or selfishness, decided to restore your name.

He asked the Church to review your case knowing

an honest court would see the terrible shame.

In nullifying your trial, they affirmed that everything

you had done had been done in God's name.

*F*or a third time, your life had been completely

examined, leaving no doubt about all that you were.

Perhaps it was part of God's plan, so later generations

would know exactly and not have to infer.

If such is the case, then it gives one pause, knowing

you suffered just to give us a record to refer.

*D*own through the ages, you have continued to live in the hearts and souls of the badly oppressed. Whether they fight corrupt governments or spiritual foes, they know you understand their protest. Standing tall as a symbol of resistance, you give hope of ultimate victory for all similarly blessed.

*W*hat, then, can sum up your life any better than your final words, calling God to you from above? In fighting tyranny, you took up your cross and followed in His footsteps out of your abiding love. Your life reminds us that the only true freedom we will ever know is given through Christ's love.

68

*T*hank you, dear maid, for teaching me

God's truths that can often be so difficult to see.

You showed through your life how to serve

Him best, in a World so full of treachery.

For all of this and all that you still are,

I will love you forever and for all eternity.

✝ Jhus maria

Bibliography

Paine, Albert Bigelow. *Joan of Arc, Maid of France.* New York: Macmillan, 1925.

Pernoud, Régine. *Joan of Arc by Herself and Her Witnesses.* New York: Stein & Day, 1966.

Pernoud, Régine. *Joan of Arc: Her Story.* New York: St. Martin's Press, 1998.

Twain, Mark (Samuel Langhorn Clemens). *Personal Recollections of Joan of Arc.* New York: Harper's, 1897.

Winwar, Frances. *The Saint & the Devil.* New York: Harper & Brothers, 1948.

Printed in the United States
149846LV00001B/25/A

9 780975 265628